GENTEFICATION

GENTEFICATION

Antonio de Jesús López

Four Way Books

Tribeca

gen·tri·fi·ca·tion (noun)
jentrəfə'kāSH(ə)n
from the Anglo root,
1.   the process of renovating and improving a house or district so
        that it conforms to middle-class taste.
2.   the process of making a person or activity more refined or
        polite.

gen·te·fi·ca·tion (a way of being)
/pronounce it como quieras/

1.   when gentrification
        becomes personal,
        and the poet as native subject
        must invade language itself,
        when mobility
        just isn't enough,
        and the poet must populate
        the canon itself
        from within;

2.   when the poet finally decides
        to smuggle a metate inside English
        & por fin beat the shards
        that've barbed his mouth.
        and out bleeds
        from barrio stone,
        this molcajete alchemy;

3.   stained saints of glass,
        fluent in the language
        of cut.

Library of Congress Cataloging-in-Publication Data

Names: López, Antonio, 1994- author.
Title: Gentefication / Antonio Lopez.
Description: New York : Four Way Books, [2021] |
Identifiers: LCCN 2021005296 | ISBN 9781945588969 (paperback)
Subjects: LCGFT: Poetry.
Classification: LCC PS3612.O583 G46 2021 | DDC 811/.6--dc23
LC record available at https://lccn.loc.gov/2021005296

This book is manufactured in the United States of America and printed on acid-free paper.

Four Way Books is a not-for-profit literary press. We are grateful for the assistance
we receive from individual donors, public arts agencies, and private foundations.

Funding for this book was provided in part by a generous donation
in memory of John J. Wilson.

This publication is made possible with public funds from the
New York State Council on the Arts, a state agency.

We are a proud member of the Community of Literary Magazines and Presses.

Contents

Notes

Introduction
by Gregory Pardlo

Imagine a world where poems radiate from the page in electromagnetic waves and readers have to use a specialized radio to capture their meaning. Imagine that for ages readers were given standard-issue radios capable of tuning in a few frequencies, and the Makers of Poems wrote in compliance with those frequencies approved by the Makers of Radios. Occasionally, some rogue Makers of Poems would use an unsanctioned frequency, and new readers would have to fashion their own radios to enjoy the work until that signal grew in strength and the Makers of Radios officially recognized the new frequency. Instead of building radios with larger, more inclusive bandwidths, however, the Makers of Radios made separate devices to capture each new frequency in isolation. Before I get even more carried away with this allegory, I want to make one point explicit: It's easy for our analogous readers, who are often Makers of Poems, to assume that the frequency they get on their standard-issue radios—because that signal is so powerful—is in some way superior to the others. Now imagine the delight, the enthusiasm, the verve and exuberance of a poet shedding that burdensome belief. Imagine the poet breaking into full flower, and marshalling the complement of cultural resources at their disposal to capture their culturally multivalent interior life. This is what awaits us in Antonio López 's debut poetry collection, *Gentefication*. When poets collapse perceived difference between discursive registers as López does, we readers have to bring multiple frames of reference to the poems, and we may have to use them all at once.

In *Gentefication*, López adorns novelty with innovation by rendering the reader—in addition to the objective world—in surprising new ways. As if they were exorcising our demons or, less ominously, assigning us roles that break from the typecast routines of our daily lives, these poems call to the surface aspects of ourselves that we are rarely asked to engage. Poems tender and ironic, earnest and outraged display a mind abundant with knowledge yet desperate for answers. While so much American poetry asks of the reader only their passive attention, these poems work like personal trainers. They call for the kind of mental and emotional absorption that can make prayer feel productive.

I look forward to a time when there will be no need to describe a poet's work as "unapologetic," a compliment that reads as a little backhanded because it raises suspicion that the poet might have had some reason to apologize. Consider, for example, how passages like, "Que tal si rezaría al-fatihah/during las posadas," interweave Spanish and English as well as Catholic and Islamic references. The poems explore such an embracing global consciousness that these references are as necessary as the legs on the stool where the storyteller is perched before us. Woven throughout *Gentefication* we are regaled with a love story, a conversion narrative and a scholarship boy's bildungsroman. While no single narrative stays faithful to the conventions those genres imply, each is a necessary dimension in the pursuit of what amounts to no less than a spiritual journey.

López is decidedly *not* code-switching here. In other words, he is not self-consciously modulating between languages, dialects and registers: the language is all of a piece. López explores the ways we are mutually intelligible at a time in our history when public discourse has been weaponized to make us presume we are cut off from one another, isolated in our social and political bubbles, and that we have no shared stories to magnify our bond. "Gente" and "gentry" share etymological roots. They are cousins, so to speak, both words evoking family and clan, people sharing a similar birth, despite the latter word's pompous sense. From "gentry," of course, we get "gentrification," the process by which a more privileged population supplants a disempowered one, a process often compared to colonialism. Martinican poet Aimé Césaire coined the word "thingification" to describe what the machine of colonialism does to human beings. In *Gentefication*, López doesn't only reverse that process by recognizing humanity on an individual level, these poems build community, an ever-expanding circle of "my people." The poems bristle with history in service of the future they imagine.

Gentefication is not all kumbaya and Whitman-like multitudes. López doesn't hesitate to throw military-grade shade. We should take to heart the "Aztec adage" the poet facetiously imparts in "Las Chácharas I Carried." "It takes 3 seconds," López reminds us, "to google my shit." Context and sentiment can transcend linguistic and cultural barriers, but when they don't, we have the tools at hand to aid us. All we need, as I say, is the will to use them.

By the time you are thirty,
you have been through a certain kind of mill . . .
—James Baldwin

"Is the American Dream at the Expense of the American Negro?" 1965

A Chicano's Self-Help Guide to Racial Trauma

I 'member the day I
stopped copping sentences
from Edgar Allan tipos.

I was trippin offa
bad dose of acid
-yellow textbooks.

Fue eight years ago,
cuando I cleansed my palate
of poisonous assumptions

over who owns this language.

When I first two-stepped cross
the 8-times-4-equals-the-number-of-seats
maze of our eighth grade classroom

to ask Ms. Nelson sumthin.
Her dagger-nose dipped
in an ol' *National Geographic*.

How she had to flick
her blonde bangs pa' verme.

I ran to the bathroom, maceta toda mareada,
and swerved over the porcelain face
of a toilet lid. Only to see wastewater visions:
      of septic cockroaches clogging a pipeline, middle school passage
          from here to San Quentin;

of saw-dusted stomachs that for years absorbed McDonald's
pink sludge-cent dreams;
of one-year subscription teachers, rentin brown kids for a résumé
like we's an overdue Redbox;
of bussed-out districts, so when an outbreak
of school fights hit the suburbs, I heard one of em whisper,
It only started when they came.

Desperate, I huffed up recuerdos of Papá
fumigando the front yard durazno.

And as he watered the roots
of our jus soli, I saw mis lunares
sprout along the brown hide.

Dressed in his waiter uniform,
he held four Chase checks,
all half-written, and asked,
¿Mi'jo, cómo se escribe one thousand?

Between the 'o's and the 's's
of the stub, I saw a tiny 'u'
—the dye of a lifelong debt.

I sat back down, turned
to the cholo scribes
who tore Webster

-Merriam, his spine
of syllable, and sentenced
McNair's only white boy

to the ballpoint arrows
of *Sur XIII*
and *Norte XIV.*

I pawed the letters,
wore their shreds
'round my stomach.

And like Apá, the OG's
before me, learned
to walk this country

with the weight
of a padded vest.

To brace my guts
for the glare of gringas,
whose prep school noses
crinkled at mis frijoles.

Ugh, what died?

How I'd leaf my skin
to the 't's, to page
my clap-back,

*The **times**
you still live in.*

Deadass, I bent over that shitter,
till I finally saw the first chunks
of industrial-sized tumors
spewing the piso—

y les cuento,
I've been spitting the rest out
ever since.

Course Description

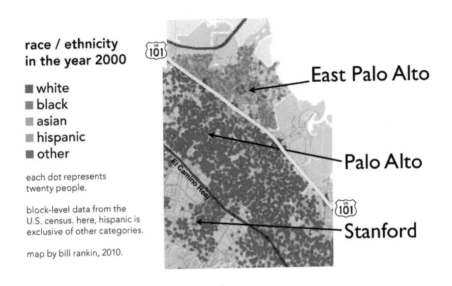

race / ethnicity in the year 2000

- white
- black
- asian
- hispanic
- other

each dot represents twenty people.

block-level data from the U.S. census. here, hispanic is exclusive of other categories.

map by bill rankin, 2010.

East Palo Alto

Palo Alto

Stanford

El Camino Real

Parts of an Ese: Theorizing Gentrification in Post-Chicano Renaissance Literature

Keywords: Silicon Desert, *Get Out* for Mexicans, Elinguation as a Second Language, Phantom Tongue

I.

It seems impossible to definitively mark the beginning of gentrification, but perhaps there are two: the influx of undocumented Spaniards into Aztlán, and the contemporary displacement of minority communities by affluent, often white, ones. Such an invasion of the VC (venture conquistador) is routinely downplayed, even by progressive media outlets. As one PBS article, "What is Gentrification?" rhetorically asked, "Who wouldn't want to see reduced crime, new investment in buildings and infrastructure, and increased economic activities in their neighborhoods?" Instead of spending hours digging up this white gaze—rooted front yards inside hedge funds—this class slips out of the suburban plots of ruin. That is, students will flee the fenced discourses of gentrification, which cage the conversation to strictly geographic terms. We will cross the cultural and psychosomatic Sonoras of English exile, into a space Chicana feminists coined "The Borderlands"—into tierras once numbed.

Las Chácharas They Carried

"¿Señora, qué declara?"

1. Discount shaving cream.

2. Tortillas wrapped in black plastic bags.

3. The telephone number of USCIS.

4. Vaporub, which in Spanish
    translates to "comprehensive
    health care."

5. My child's nosebleed.

"What's the intention of your visit?"

6. My son who stirs awake,
    as the Nyquil's starting to wear off.

7. Father's sombrero that I promised
    to never take off the wall.

"If I search your vehicle, will I find anything?"

8. Soap camouflaged
    as sea salt.

9. La madrugada
    whose bordertown haze
    stains Mother's dress.

10.   An analog TV set
        to plop my chubby brown hijo
        in front of *Sesame Street* . . .

"Ma'am, please step outside."

The Last Day My Father Spent in México

At eighteen, Apá cleans tables at Hyatt restaurants with imported sweat. He smuggles his wife and two children into Sunday brunch, where I've learned with a nun's piety to stop calling him Papá in public. Apá bites his tongue under every "Pick it up," and "Excuse me, señor," grunted amidst clanking silverware. He sees the chalk of clients' white fingers snapping the outline of EPA crime scenes, the underside of an aguacate which bears the same skin as un cuerno de chivo, the auto-defensas and carteles still patrolling the plazas de Michoacán. While on this side of North America, he sees the avocado is trending, hollowed out so white people can mine its green gold to make caramel lattes.

This morning, Apá pours greasy caldo over a cazuela of chiles rellenos. We huddle over the bonfires of an almuerzo in a small apartment with three plastic chairs, but six different pictures of the Virgin Mary. My grandfather naps, his wife tugs at una gelatina. As she struggles to peel off the pegamento, she sighs, "Eres el único hijo que aún manda dinero."

At fifty-two, Apá lowers a sack of Maseca as a doorstop, so his parents can shuffle their feet across the carpet and open the door—so they can cross the threshold, and properly despedirse de él.

Primaria

Because when Tío first cried,
I was already a man.

Porque aquí, lo que gana uno diario
es un mes en México.

Because when his family left
and he had to stay, we numbed
our lips with Fruit Loops.

Because when homeboys bent down
to tie their shoes, one of us
made a slurping sound.

Because Christian wore his shorts
a little too tight.

Because we all thought Mr. Ross
was just being friendly to the girls.
Because Mrs. Ross changed
her last name.

Because in Disney movies,
we're always Chihuahuas.

Because when Darius and I dapped
—plum elbows shot up
from his shirt—
my chest flushed.

Because childhood was women
trying on tacones.

And Vane laughed when I said,
The yellow pair looks cute.

Las Chácharas I Carried (Translated from the Mexican)

The customs agent switched his nightstick
for a number two pencil and asked at workshop,

"I'm not sure what this word means here.
Does anyone know?"

1.   A cutting board to butcher
my tongue, and hope bleeding's
a universal language.

2.   A bilingual dictionary—kept abreast
like the Khan family's pocket Constitution.

3.   The English word for the Aztec adage:
"It takes three seconds to google my shit."

4.   A book of poems to hand
my father, the edges smeared
in molcajete and refried beans.

5.   My tears
as Apá strains
his chords
to read
my hymns
for him.

6.   An ink made of his cook orders.

7.   His baby blue dress shirt to wear
       at my MFA thesis defense.

8.   The declaration,
       "It'll be in ambos idiomas."

9.   A voice recorder to replay his voice
       inside the hollow walls of my Newark apartment
       till I finish singing the Barrio Beatitudes.

10.   His question, "¿Hijo,
       cuándo vas a regresar?"

la pelea

golden boy lands a hook!
i take un trago y grito,
but spit up an english

that now tastes
like flat beer.

i cup
tío nacho's modelo,
its sweating neck numbs
mis dedos, & jam

my chewed nail
under the tab, sip

the drunken chants,

the malted honey
that teems my tongue

to pry open

the bronze-kissed mouths
who've waged all week
for the grainless display
of pay-per-view.

i watch the pixel
fireflies that light up
their sawdust boots.

they stand by
mexican ringside—
the backyard botanas
of tajín'd pepinos
& dying charcoal.

slouched at the ready
for de la hoya to swing
at sugar shane.

i lean back,
recite las chispas
de frases that brush off
their bigotes,

& hope to land
a sentence.

La Reina de Tejas (Live from the Astrodome)

Amá said you died the week before I was born,
que eras tan feroz with your jumper,
before se puso de moda, and the little girls who wore 'em

butterflew into muchachas. Tenía que verte
in pot-bellied teles, canal crackling
like comal-burnt tortillas. Te ví

in pants flared like your nariz, chata
like my sister's. I munched on tacos, juice
dripping as Amá squealed, *Agarra la colita.* Te ví

your hands castanets, my size 3 Godzilla shoes
tapped to their bidi bidi. Tus eyebrows arched
to a dome with tierra-dusked faces. Te ví

como la flor la maestra Barragán showed us,
a night-blooming cactus I called *selena
grandiflorus.* From Tejana lips, ví

the Spanish I couldn't mouth. Stuttered songs
till words flowed like the taco's orange grasa.
I lick my fingers, lean on the couch cover. Ví

you peer from orange-stained glass, cooing
my tongue to finally sing, *Me diste túúúú.*
My heart trembled, *I can speak like us.* Ví,

full lips like mine hush the roaring crowd
that tightens my tummy just like Amá's
raspberry kisses. You leave the stage,

your sparkles sugar the sofa's puddle of drool.

Cheat Code to Second Base

When Rosemary smiles at me, it makes my cheeks hurt,
like when I eat a sour strawberry.

Her curls are bob-webs, slivers of sombra
whirled into each other.

Lost in their own loops, like when we make
human knots in P.E.

She fixes a scrunchie on her back, so a medium white
tee hugs her curves.   "Hey."

I dig my foot in the woodchips, heartbeats away
from her leopard sandals.

I stare at Michael, the homie in all things
Resident Evil.

He cranes his neck to my starchy collar,
"Chill, I gotchu."

Our Pokémon Stadium debates dribble across
the hallway,

where thirty-two pairs of brown and black hands
bang poles, chipping

at the well-fed coats of turquoise. My mind shuffles
through how to defeat

a Psychic type: *If Wobbuffet uses Mirror Coat,*
then Mewtwo will strike firs—

And Rosemary's freckles burst in my face
like polvorones,

"Did you just slap my ass?"

She looks at me, me looks at Michael.
He just be laughin

at the smack he gave my hand, gettin clammy
from what it's lost:

I imagined we'd kiss behind the portables,
me stuttering to touch

her jeans' back pocket. The other 6th graders yell
"MOVE" But she doesn't.

She just looks cold—her eyes the color
of chocolate milk.

Handwashing Instructions at a Unisex Bathroom

1.   Wet

Place hands inside
Southpole pockets.

"H-hey."   "Hey."
"So, what do we do?"   "Whatever you want."

Practice on a caseless pillow.
Wake to a bulged screwdriver
and froths of premature

2.   Soap

The morning of, Urban Dictionary her text,
"FWB." "Friends with benefi—"
Put down the SAT flashcards.

                              "Abject"
                              "Abnegation"
                              Suck her.

                    Crouch
              con knees
          shaking

like a newborn
        calf's.

        The tiles laugh

at your form.

Throw her leg
on the handicap rail,
till she moans,

"I have a condom."

Don't be a stereotype and say
you don't know.

3.   Rinse

With fingernails still bitten,
rasp her tender walls.

"Agh, it hurts."
Switch to pinkie, feel

the throbbing stalactite.
As her white mocos clump,

ask yourself, *do you even want to—*
Shut up!   *All boys*   *wanna.*

Pull her closer, so lotus flower
meets your nopalito.

I can't get it up.
Me mira con piedad.

Puedo subirlo.   Think of girls
you've watched on Monday Night Raw.

I can't get it up!

"You going in or what?"   Grunt.   "Yeah."
"My legs are getting tired."   Grunt.   "Sorry."

She fastens her zipper,
"It's fine."

4.   Dry

The question
that sweats
your lips,

"Did that count
as your first?"

How to Lose a Misdebeaner

"Fabian Zaragoza of East Palo Alto appeared in San Mateo County Superior Court on charges of murder with the special circumstance of lying in wait, two counts of attempted murder with infliction of great bodily injury and use of a firearm in connection with the shooting that killed 3-month-old Izack Jesus Jimenez Garcia and wounded his parents. If convicted, Zaragoza could face life in prison without the possibility of parole . . . He did not enter a plea Wednesday, and his arraignment was held over until next week . . . He turns 18 in December." —*SFGate*, June 8, 2011

1.   From the Deposition

      a.   A sixth grade Pokémon card-swap
                  at his house—a block from mine:

      b.   *Aight, I'll give you my Shiny Charizard*
                  for those legendaries you got!

                  Naw blood, you call that a fair trade?
                  These two are Kanto region. 1ˢᵗ edition.

      c.   *Bruh, I been seen that Charizard!*
                  TWENTY bucks at la pulga!

                  You wuffin! Veinte dólares mi culo!

      d.   *Bet. Tell you what, how bout...*

2.   Arraignment

      a.   Your Honor, lemme chew
                  his life-sentence. Slowly.
                  Like the stale hot dogs
                  we'd eat for lunch.

      b.   The Tongan lunch lady
                  bribed our hunger

with another bag
of Cheesy Doritos

when we complained,
The buns got mold in 'em.

3.   DNA Evidence

   a.   If the jury can turn their heads
         to his pumped stomach,
         you'll notice the last bits
         of a granola bar—

         king-size & studded
         in chocolate chips,

   b.   As you'll see from the tape,
         each kid opens his hands
         to the passing milk crates
         hulled from the lunch hall

   c.   (Cuz they only brought the good stuff
         for the STAR test.)

4.   Dress Code

   a.   C-walk inside a small taqueria.
         La cajera's trippin' that I brought
         the pale statue that is Tommy.

b.   He imports the greased-up tortillas
into his Old World mouth.

c.   As we eat, my sis calls me,
my mouth mid-rábano,

Fabián's trial, it's today!
And don't you even think about goi—

d.   We race to San Mateo Superior Court,
already flanked by Univisión
and ABC news vans—
a bilingual alliance to interview

my tatted up ex-classmates
who stand like Egyptian guards
at the throat of the door.

e.   *Naw we ain't here to start sum shit.*
We jus goin see him to the end.

f.   We pass the metal detectors,
the Escher-looking escaleras,
to a room que parece a las misas

he'll never see.

5.   Pardon

  a.   The teary-eyed mother who curses
        at Fabián, my beardless felon,
        Where are your parents?!

  b.   This blonde-locked wonder
        next to me, seeing it all
        with the calmest of eyes.

  c.   This pinche güero,
        who stopped me from seeing
        Fabián speak for the last time
        as a free boy.

  d.   My one white friend
        who didn't know,
        *You can't bring shorts
        to court.*

  e.   My mind that leaps from seeing
        his navy-and-white school uniform
        to this orange jumpsuit,

        where his name is ciphered
        across his chest two-ways:

  f.   On the left, six numbers.
        On the right, his initials—

        1.   Hereafter, D.O.C.

Learning Goals

II.

This course standstills on the homophonic collapse when the *ese* must, like his Mexican parents once did, tuck his body inside the *essay*—the vehicle for mobility into el norte's universe/ities. This poem is interested in the moment when Mr. Connors lifted his fine-tipped tongue over my personal statement, waxed the school's signet on my hairless chest. The collection relives the heat, the heat I felt when across the polished oak he beamed, "You have a bright future ahead of you." It hears the quiet rattle of Mrs. Wynters, who as she presented the library's top prize, lowered her glasses to this spectacle, "So how did you *escape* East Palo Alto?" This award-winning debut won't forget her eyes, their blue-eyed ink which seared my skin like a Chicano tattoo. This body swallows the day I tried to speak back, but the applause flooded my mouth.

The Disciples of San Mateo County, California

And God said to Juventino:
perform ablution over the bathroom sink,
          press the cold metal with novice palms.
Stretch out your double white tee, the cotton bullet-
          proof vest where upon stepping
in the schoolyard, you'll face juvenile
          punches. Brace the iron gaits
with knock-off Cortezes. Cuff your sagging
          Dickie's by the ankles. Saunter
through the cracked voices of boys who laugh
          without a tag for their torsos.
Unzip your brother's fur jacket,
          and take Father's flask. Drink from
his Patrón. Shadowbox the heavy
          gavel-swings, with swigs of your own.
Cleanse yourself in liquor's kerosene,
          let flammable spirits purge
all nerves. To be an acolyte, embalmed
          in hair gel, worshipping
the altars cordoned off in caution tape,
          is sainthood.

Triptych of the Adobe-Cotta Army
East Palo Alto, circa 2000 A.D.

My fingers are desperate
to unearth the ruins
of my countrymen.

Only to find a Tesla
on the second floor
of our apartments

—now a parking garage.

The Amazon logo
smirks above me
like a biblical cloud.

*

Out here, hooded saints
tore the covenant
of earthly silence.

Passed out Zig-Zag
leaflets, to preach
the gospel of skin.

Whirling dervishes
in long white tees
bum-rushed me

at a bautizo, pressed
against my lips
a cholo's chalice.

My chest flushed
at watching boys bronze
into adobe-cotta.

A driveway floodlight,
the barrio's moon,
cast their bodies

as they placed bets
against the armors they carried.
A fist tucked

inside a hoodie,
his knuckles spelling
the names of ex-lovers.

Each letter tatted
with a paper clip.
Cocked belt buckle

whose colors shout
to the block
who he fucks with,

until asphalt swallows
him again. And Marías
now mourn Jesús

outside a sagging fence,
wreathe his chain-
link with lit candles,

cardboard signs saying
"We miss you," streamers
without the heated balloon

that promised flight.

*

Consider the clothesline as a bandolier

slung over ruined soldiers,
whose uniformes still cling
onto apartment balconies.

Quien cedieron sus tierras
to raise the wrinkled flags
of blusas and neon vests.

Consider this Aztec sacrifice:
a father offers an empire
his daily flesh. Kneels

on the melted tar
of its tongue, winces
at the body turned legal (tender).

All to nurse the newborn
with this vision,
Una vida mejor.

And so Father cradled my head
inside asphalt. Prayed
for our rite

to simply wade.

sideshow
after danez smith & e-40

& on his day off, god said, *shake dem dreads!* bolts rain from braided
crowns. & this the first time i hear thunder. *count the mississippis* like
pbs said, the fresh-to-death disciples that flint the blacktop with dabs—
lightning hands that'd make cassius blush. & after using up all his sick
days, the lord chants, *go stupid!* miguel hands me a four loko. i sniff the
dixie's lip, when homeboy yells, ándale bruh! the pulque drips down
my nostrils. & under this freeway bridge, i vision when he first swap-
met his feather headdress for a raiders cap. & after not even showin
up to work, the most high blasts, *now watch em swang!* apostles snatch
my hairless arms & summon me to two-step atop a toyota. from the
hood, car & kid jekyll into stainless gamblers, bettin whose chassis will
cave in first from the stomps of tims & a 12's boot. & after puttin up
his 2 weeks, god throws that slap back. *ghost-ride the whip!* & my heart
thumps with that good shit. i confess to an og, *im trippin rogue*. it's
father darius from mt. olive a.m.e. he quotes a verse from the book of
friday. Aw man, that's jus the chronic. fine honeys latch onto butterfly
doors, the blk chevy in fronta me screeches at the scent of burnt tires
& 4-inch pumps. & on his last day, god emcees the whole damn thing.
now gas break dip dip! little mans slide thru, ridin on they scraper bikes
cuz the sky was taken. & after that, god dont member shit, but deandre
recorded the rest. suposably, jesús grabbed the rest of the fifth, climbed
atop the roof of an ac transit—oakland's tallest sinai—& straight dissed
his old man. *tell me when to go!*

Letter to the Editor

Dara Kerr
C|Net
235 Second St.
San Francisco, CA 94105

September 15, 2015

Dear Ms. Kerr,

Last month, your colleagues cut a measly ribbon, patted themselves on the back for gifting us a new health clinic. The press bravely announced East Palo Alto as a "strategic location" in the Silicon Valley, and widely touted tech hubs like Facebook, Google, and NASA Ames Research for being on the "cutting edge of social innovation."

In your article, "Life on the Other Side of the Silicon Valley's Tracks," you sprinkled phrases like "we paid a visit to this once down-and-out" town.

But there are few glaring questions your article leaves out:
1. How come I didn't have one white friend till I was sixteen?
2. How come I thought his private school was the White House?
3. Why did Atherton moms keep asking if I was related to the facilities workers?
4. Should I unlearn Spanish so I can take the SAT II "fairly"?
5. How many times does my dad have to make pozole for PTA meetings?

Más que nada, cómo te parace if you and your colleagues wrote about *us,* and not just the negative shit?

Sincerely,

a lifelong resident

After I take my Shahada,
November 20, 2015

Rashid pops his Chevy '08 & offers me
a cloth. Its silk thirsts in the imported oil
of his fingers. I unfurl the Moroccan cloth,
& I'm a flower boy again. My salted petals
ensnared the mariachi, guiding trumpets
to cry inside my chest. The singing brass
melted my torso as a stuttering trompo
who slipped from the strings of Papá
& skidded onto la plaza. My legless body
grew the steel tips, zapatearon los nervios
away. The brothers shout *Allahu Akbar,*
& I am anointed to dervish. & I too
hear the whirs when my forehead
meets sajjada, & chants God's name.

The Hadith of Gabriel: (Mexican) Muslim's Version
Mawlid al-Nabi (September 23, 2015)

Tell me about Islam,

          el arcángel asked the Prophet.
    & I ask Abdul, as he paints luces verdes
        around a mini Ka'Ba.

        I pick a brush too, but all I see
    are fourth grade Mission Projects.

Habibi, tell me about iman.

          ¿Que tal si rezo Al-fatihah
    during las posadas,

        where mamás wait with ollas
    outside their doors, peleando
        por el mejor ponche?

          Where even the children hush
    under mango trees.

Akhi, what if I sang las mañanitas

        to the Prophet, mustered
    my best Chente? "Estas soooon las
        mañanitas que cantaban al nabi."

        The ears of Rasul Allah
    tickled by the frayed tassels
        of my Arabic.

Sadiqi, tell me of the Hour

when my feet touch
Rawalpindi, & mis huaraches press
the red-and-green chalk.

When I see a son who holds
the Pakistani flag, like las chiquillas
en secundaria who marched

en la cancha. Y las guardias
de escolta cried,
"¡Paso corto!"

When Father and I walk
inside Grand Jamia Mosque,
& Arabi sutures
the lines between fingers.

When I can count dhikr,
& teach Apá to open his palms.

To wash his tough hands
with the names
of a faceless God.

When I no longer tremor
in the garage, at hearing
Apá's footsteps.

When I start praying
with my eyes closed,
    & open them to him
drawing holy water

    from the font
        in my eyes.

Thieves of Light
November 18, 2016

Rashid ends the khutbah
    with his favorite story.
    I used to shoot some Shaytan

    into the ledge of my veins. Till
    off the seventh floor of our trap,
    Rasul Allah came in my sleep.

    He ordered me to build a masjid,
    not just in East Orange, but 'cross
    Garden Liquors! Down the street!

    Now alhamdulillah, our brothers
    keepin' they paychecks. And err'y Friday,
    we sit cross-legged in fronta these here rehals.

    We don't move our heads to bottles,
    blunts, or fast women. Nuthin' but
    the words of the Most High.

    A'ight, 'nuf of me.
    Aqeemu as-Salah.

A grunt faintly trims the air,
    the imam's weekly taper,
    Fellas, keep the lines straight.

We real flossed in Friday's best
    thobes. Standing shoulder-
    to-shoulder in Nike socks.

The shoe rack's gagged
with flea-market Tims
& retro-fitted high tops.

I slip off my Air Force Chanclas,
& swerve past the dusty tarps.

.

*

I bought my bootleg'd dīn
        in downtown Newark,
        where Al-Fatihah blasts
        outside a Dollar Tree.

    Where God breathes
    through manhole covers.

    And *Ebony* temples
    stand over subwoofers
    to hawk off beard oils.

My bootleg'd dīn's held
        by Brick City's pillars,
        as thieves of light bump
        they heads to dark-tinted
        throwbacks.

    Thumm.
            Thumm.

Thumma kallā
        sawfa ta`lamūna

My bootleg'd dīn prays
        to the qibla of bodegas,

                where vices rank-and-file
                the block like a lineup.

                Pigs on the beat,
                sniffing for signs of last night's
                idol worship.

Outside the mosque, a Dutchmaster sticks
        out the shirt pocket of a Boricua.

                It's Don Ramón,
        y ya tiene two strikes
                from broken taillights
        and broken English.

A crowd gathers at the back
        of his rusted blue Honda:
                Lupe's peluche three weeks overdue
                        for build-a-bear surgery.
                Her stickers from doctor visits
                        fill the back window.
                Emilio's glow-in-the-dark cleats
                        rest atop a gutted seat.

Still, the K-9 squad licks
        its fangs, suspects lunch
        came early.

Behind me, the mosque rattles.
        I turn and see Rashid
        shadow over the padlock.

El Morisco

After she finds out, Amá buries her face
        in the sky-colored sheets
of my bedroom. Rubs her tears
        with her Home Depot apron.

Tu papá me llamó en su break.
¡¿No te importa?!

        ¡Claro que sí!

I reach her shoulders, knead
        through forty-six years
of tender flesh, searching
        for those words,

al final del día, eres mi hijo.
        Instead, she bursts,
¿Pero por qué lo hiciste?

I sob into the knock-off Borealis
        of my cell's screensaver. Tears blur
the Spanish Wikipedia page of Islam.
        I read for her, for me, for anything
but this maldito silencio.

        ¿Quéres que yo lea más?
No.

Quiero decirle que catecismo beat
        the devotion out of me. That I found

49

more of God in the doorless parlors
        of eloteros and churro vendors,

in the sizzling lime of repurposed
        produce bags, than in the fifty-foot
pews of a Yosemite-sized Christ.
        Que encontré more of the most high

        in the soup kitchen's atoles,
in Father Goode's teeth getting stuck
        while chewing a pan dulce oreja
than in reciting seis misterios

        in la sala's strangling light
as we huddled around a fake chimney
        with Abuela kneeling on
the crumbling limestone.

I grab the silver-leafed bible
        on my bottom shelf. Paw
its fat crucifix, the olive branches
        that laurel the cover.

Madre, te prometo que trataré
        de fortalecer mi fé.
Iré a misa más,
        hablaré con los sacerdotes.

I cup her fist with both hands.
      Cualquier cosa que pidas
de mí, lo haré. Sólo dame
      tu bendición.

But I see it—her choked-up throat
      that chips away
at la lengua's levee,
      so the dammed grief

of a lost son trembles
      on her lip.
A muddied English spills
      onto the sheets.

Son, what didn't our religion
      offer you?

Texts

III.

Habibti, let's take inventory:

3 hours per night spent over the phone, falling asleep
        to your confession.
2 months talking.
4 visits to the mosque.
$68 spent on Uber Select (cuz I didn't know the difference).
A 25-cent gumball machine that popped
        in the middle of our walks
        around Southpoint mall.
6 cheap-ink brochures on the faith.
1 trip to Harris Teeter
        donde me miraste, asked my name
        not as a question, but to see
        how it tasted on your lips.

Convert Glossary

Tabula Rasa: Latin for I first prayed
        on a used bath towel.

Salaam: to shake after months filled
        with fitna, the cloro'd hands
of a Honduran convert,
        cuarenta cuaresmas old.

Shukr: when I lent him my tasbih
        for a lifetime, in honor of wiping
hospital floors; of staying
        after every jumu'ah

        to put away chairs.

Tajweed: the way he pronounced
        Fa-yet-vil,
the Carolina city
        donde tomó su testigo.

Sujud: when an egret bends its mouth
        inside a sea,

        the cheap incense
of sin that singes his MEChAs,
        as he learns to drink

from the Qur'an's ink.

Tawbah: to claw towards repentance,
        like los peregrinos en la Basílica
de Guadalupe;

        like the legless man
inside this masjid
        who bends over his wheelchair.

Istighfar: to clothe my loneliness
        with a pair of lace panties, join
the drowned hornets who floated
        atop red cups, guzzled

all the pineapple chunks
        of this dunya; to betray
You, skip salah tantas veces;

these dedos that groped for moans,
        now count Your names;

        my beads of sweat that thread
this negligee neglect.

An-Nikah
June 18, 2016

Her brother's voice sings in my ribcage.
You gon' do this, right?

Pienso en ese día, where she played
with the inside of my blue flannel,

Aw shit, the sleeves getting loose.
and I caught her henna-handed.

The music between us, as she plucked
each string from her abaya. She looked

at me, and somewhere between a joke
and jab, said, *Honestly, I ain't really been*

into Mexicans before. Seven months later,
I'm inside this mosque, where curly-headed

Luqman ushers me into a satin red room,
musters his high school Spanish,

trátala bien. He sits next to their father
and his hard-earned blessing.

She's dressed like La Virgen,
green shawl haloes her body.

Holding my hand, she leads me to sign
An-Nikkah. The sisters giggle at the convert-

turned-man, whose fingers fumble in the maze
of Arabic to find his name on the dotted line.

My eyes leave the document. The letters bleed
into the room, which is no longer a room,

but an inked sea that surges from the table. I wade
for the shades of black to ebb, for uncles to shout

takbir. But the thirty-something eyes just read me
stuttering over the fine print of Islam—to the terms:

> *Leave Amrika.*
> *Apply for Emirati citizenship.*
> *Embrace Baba's oil money.*
> *Teach English to diplomat children*
> *(mine will probably lose their Spanish).*

> *Amá.   Apá.   México.   Michoacán.*

> *Allah,*
> > *what did you do with Dios?*

> *¿Dónde lo pusiste?*

> *In EE.UU?   In U.A.E.?*

*

56

My bootleg'd dīn threatened
to steal me. Swallow me whole.

I softly press my hands against hers,
and confess,

Querida, I can't do this.
Isn't it me that's supposed to get cold feet?

I'm serious. Err'thing's too mixed up.   *With me.*
I don't understand . . .

I take the breath I couldn't give her.

No puedo orar
a dos dioses.

What's that mean?

I let the Spanish fill
the air. To ease me

into breaking the house
I've dreamt with her.

I can't . . .
worship

I look at her one last time.
Her freckles are the stars in Mt. Hira.

Two gods.

Goddess Tonantzín

At her halo, Ilhuícatl-Meztlí.
Sky and moon frolic
under God's cloudy cornea.

At her waist, the stars
wept with each
lift of hem

in rickety streets,
where even the broom-
fingers of grandmas

can't reach.

At her feet lie the hills
of Tepeyac, which translates
to "nose-mountain,"

where I breathe the myrrh
of burning maize husks
and backyard fogones.

Where every twelfth of December,
bodies are hallowed out like a reed flute:
    coyolli attached to adobe limbs—
        each chime of their ankle seed
        stirs ribbons of reverent smoke;
    orejas la caracola
        that hermit to divine call.

When I close my eyes,
I feel the dīn's cloak,
unable to tell if it's
a tilma or an abaya.

And I see La Virgen whisper to Juan Diego,
Fill your cloak with roses. Open it
before the bishop. His stately Holiness,
unable to cope with the weight
of a single rose, will lay down
his crozier, and kneel to the image
imprinted in your cotton.

I see Muhammad run to Khadija.
Cover me! Cover me! She wraps
her robe around his skin,

so that in the arms of beloved,
the forty-year-old Prophet
is but a child.

Between my fingers
is a veil through which
I may glimpse the sun—

a burning star
that, still in dull fajr,
waters my eyes.

Which Cobija Feels Most Comfy?: A Letter to Nabra

"The murder of a teenage Muslim girl beaten and killed by a bat-wielding motorist near a Virginia mosque was likely a 'road rage incident,' not a hate crime, US police said, prompting outrage from many who say the teen was targeted because of her religion. Darwin Martínez Torres, 22, has been arrested and charged with Nabra Hassanen's murder in an incident police say began as a road dispute with a male teenager who was among Hassanen's group." —*Al Jazeera*, June 20, 2017

As-Salamu Alaykum, Sister.

The papers said
road rage,
your death

as no more taxing
than a busted taillight.
Like when they said

Deah, Yusor, Razan's
were a *parking dispute*.
Hermanita, I've spent

the past four days
whispering your name
with hands cut

by the blades
of grass that pillow
your hair, with hands

willowed in dua.
But my palm lines fled
to trace their ancestry

elsewhere. Across the Atlantic,
to the Birth of a Nation's Nation,
where the ghoulish white hood

of a van drove into Finsbury Park,
shouting, *I WANT TO KILL
ALL MUSLIMS!*

And for the first time, I saw
an Islamic extremist.
Imam Mohamed Mahmoud

protects the suspect
from the mob, and issues
an anti-Western fatwa,

*We pushed people away . . .
until he was safely taken
by police. . . .*

Imam Mahmoud, who professed
to *Sky News, I am no hero.*
But then who is ours?

Ya Allah, I beamed
for a DC Comics adhan
to call some sunnah superhero.

But there's no star-spangled
shield to guard your glasses
and Jannah-gated smile

because Captain America
wasn't made for you.
No Wonder Woman

to deflect blind-eyed
bat swings with a buckle
of eight karats.

Sister, let me still pay
for next year's prom dress,
a mermaid lavender,

so after iftar, I'll sip chai,
and hear the fiqh disputes
of uncles slamming hairy-

knuckled gavels. *Astaghfirullah,*
there'll be boys, drinking,
your father will interrupt. *And me.*

Let me stand over the Mexican minarets
of Univisión & Telemundo
and la pinta & the bus stop

y la clínica, & the good bench
at recess, & tell el pueblo,
mi pueblo, to enshroud you

in our finest cobijas—
those linens not even
hawked at flea markets.

Let me quietly clean
tu cuerpo over el agua nacida
de la barranca, the river-

mountaintops to see
the heights my people
could've soared for you.

Let my apolog—
take a lifetime,
take *my* lifeline—

hang on this letter,   'y?'

Why must this land learn Arabic names
at the eight o'clock news?

Why must Sister Aydin write
a Facebook post warning
Muslim girls to travel in groups,

in broad daylight?

Why couldn't you finish
Ramadan first?!

Why?

                                          Why?
                  Why?

Why.

Seventeen Words, One for Every Year You Were Given

all I know
is that every Muslim
in America,

by morning,
became an atheist
to American Progress.

A Document-Based Question (DBQ)

"I remember having an argument—a most melancholy argument—with a friend of mine concerning our relation to Martin. It was shortly after our celebrated and stormy meeting with Bobby Kennedy, and I was very low. I said we could petition and petition and march and march and raise money and give money until we wore ourselves out and the stars began to moan: none of this endeavor would or could reach the core of the matter, it would change nobody's fate" —James Baldwin, *No Name in the Street* (1972)

IV.
. . . and the stars began to moan . . .

Total Time—1 hour, 30 minutes

Directions: When fleshing out the ese, consider these questions.

- When did you first learn to package your family's grief?
- Can Papá ever take off his work shoes in your poems?
- Are Juan Pablo and Devonte just statistics to cite in scholarship apps?
- Do they lay still on the autopsy of stats tables?
- Are they yours to mine?
- Do you always imagine Felix wearing his orange jumpsuit?
- Why's it now *his* jumpsuit?
- Are they all prisoners to your image?
- What violence(s) do(es) your mouth (now) harbor?
- Have the means become their own end?

Grading Rubric

Trauma is weighted as follows:

Formal Essays (55-65%)

> Write "Children of Immigrants" – 10% (double if
> undocumented)
> Write "first generation" – 15%
> Mention the color of the coyote's van – 10%
> Keep family in the past tense – 5%
> Write birthplace next to its murder per capita rate – 20%

In-Class (35%)

> Don't correct them when they say your name wrong – 5%
> Go by Tony starting sophomore year – 10%
> Stay quiet when they make fun of Keisha – 5%
> Believe Tim when he says, "You just got in because you're" – 10%
> When it's your turn to read, pronounce it like they do, *gwa-da-mala* – 5%

Participation (10%)

> Turn to the person next to you:
> debate your belonging

Source A: ESL
after Roger Reeves' "Cymothoa Exigua"

The tongue as a debut ribbon
to slice and applaud: to lose
consciousness & wake up indoors:
when the smell of cooked chicken
creeps into your nose, & teeth remember
what it means to chew: to make the mouth
a gulley for the first pale stranger
who cradles your head & says, *drink:*
when the glistening neck of his canteen
prods your lips, & words you've never heard
raid in: when the names of the room's dead
fill your throat, & bedloads of migrants
cover their children's mouths each time
they knock: when loose threads of tongue fall
on your stubby fingers, & soon you unravel
how you arrived here: to mourn the Jordans
hung on telephone wires, the muscle memories
of a coupe that stopped mid-street, a tinted face
lowers the glass curtain, & suddenly your pick-up
game's one man short: to still hear his jump shot:
when the court chuckled as his elbows locked in,
& 21's just a game, never an age reached:
when the pale stranger invites his neighbors,
how they marvel at your mouth's archaeology:

when wives paw its rot & decide to form book clubs
around your grief: when a smile lurks
in the corner of your jaw, as they proclaim you
their latest myth.

Source B: Oral Exam

At the outskirts of the estate, men laugh under dogwood. A cackling fire
sheds their skins of badges & trench coats. The mangled moon

bleeds through the sill, & grins wide as branches surround the bed.
Four scouts practice their knots on your limbs; the tallest stuffs a rag

inside your mouth. A man probes your tongue, his fingers the weight
of a cotton gin—they taste of ash, still. You can't see his face, only a hand

that lowers to his hip. And as the blade leaves its sheath, it whistles
through history. *This is for your own good boy.*   That voice.

The pale stranger bends down, presses his thumb against your lower lip,
& a hook pierces your cheek.   When the footsteps fade, you hobble

to the mirror, peel your lip which stings of the burning air.
& beneath the fleshy gash, you see   the steel.

That was after all the deal: to fix your mouth like a Mexican cock.
So that everywhere you went, you'd carry a tiny knife—

so that the only language you'd speak

was fighting.

Source C: The Memory of Hunger: A Response to Richard Rodríguez

Maestro, I am afraid that London fog will dissolve
    my champurrado heart.

That my degrees—of maestrías & doctorados—
    will be of separation.

That a debit card is braille
    for how I treated Apá:
    an Automated Toño Machine.

That Duke will bust my greaser face on a plaque,
    limón-scent their library
    with a barrio's Pledge,

pero que no he sido
    a Fabuloso son.

Richard, as marooned Mexicans, can we escape
    the Museum of Other that curated
    our bodies? Can I ignite this canon

not with gunpowder, but the sodden
    tinder of my father? Who embers,
    Acá te espero, mi campeón.

Dear Elder, quizás memory *is* a hunger,
    that twenty years later, crosses
    a pond that isn't El Rio Bravo.

But what if my father pronounces *line,* so it becomes leña
         burning inside me? So I may wade this lonely body
         of work with swarthy oars. So my accent will echo

inside Oxford Union, erode the medieval stone
         with a waiter's shoe polish, his stained-glass English
         pronouncing Marshall Scholar as, *Mi hijo es un Marcha'.*

So I am not a figure,
         but the part of Anglo speech
         whose hyphen betrays a chasm.

That is to say, un verbo mojado, a Deferred Action
         movement que trabajará en putiza
         to bridge the English Channel
         with all our dichos,
         nuestras formas de pensar.

So every sentence can feed your, & our,
         olvido.

DRA.
DACA

HIJA
SOLO
SEPA

K YO
-I-
LUV
YOU

BERI
MUCH

DARÉ
TODO

CADA
JUMX
TAMP
-ICO
INCA
COLA

JUGO
DE MI
SER,

PARA

K
QUE-
DES

JI-JI
JEIR
JEIR
HERE.

POR
N MI
S BRA-
ZOS,

HAY
NIN-
GUNA
LEY.

Mom,
I've
had
to
live
only
spic
-ing
the
four
let-

or
less
spac
DACA
gave
me.

But not anymore.

Mámi, I was
pre-diabetic.
Now, I am
pre-med.

Todo por
y para tí.

This week,
we will
study the
heart.

8 hundred
thousand
DACA-
mented
hearts

equals
3 million

chamber
valves.

All choked by
two chambers
of congress.

Our hearts pump
peso, dolar,
y euro

-pean wages.
Apá fue
un peón
de este país.

Cómo lo
extraño.

Amá,
the heart
weighs 11 ounces.

Ounces,
ounces.

Once upon
a PBS show,

I had a dream
-er. Of 1 DACA,

to open
una clínica
en cada
barrio.

That tú y yo
would start
our dietas
otra vez,
the 5th time
this week,

and you'd
hold in
your palm
2 platos de
pupusas.

I have
6 meses
to get it
renewed.

To fit in
this dress
for Vane's boda

—that I may not
even get to go to.

To pick
the best
strawberries
in the farmers'
markets

and dip them
in, like you say
it, *jerchi's*
chocolate.

Like cuando
mirabas
la cocina,
en todo un
desmadre.

And I vowed
to never wash
these hands.

And you lifted that
chancla-throwing
mano,

until tus besos
limpiaron mis

dedillos.

And we were gemelas
of syrup'd lips,

concocting a new matte.
How we'd sing
the new Selena song

until Papá
came home:

BIDI
BIDI
BALM
BALM!

Source E: Conjugations of My Tía's Back

Ella	Yo
Ay, mi espalda.	Fill a chipped white bookshelf con *The Republic* y *Madame Bovary.*
Ay, mi'jo—no ya comí gracias.	Y ay, her back hurts.
Lo sobo, y sobo, y sobo.	Debate the line break.
	Perfect its vertebrae,
Quisiera regresar a México	healthy columns.
con estos dedos de cloro, y grasa de torta.	I said her back hurts! Craft exercise 1: Use chiasmus.
	I workshop, they shop for work.
Y no, no me han llamado del consulado.	In this poem, four Mexicans have already offered to fix the stanza's roof,
¿Qué hay acá para mí?	drywall all negative space.
	My tía *breaks line,* asks for work comp.
	Craft exercise 2: Use irony.
	Her name's Dolores.

Nosotros

Saw three Mexicans
at the bus stop. Two wear
neon green, orange cones
attached to their limbs.

They fight la vejez like a
cement mixing truck.

The guy who picked
me up at Reno played
Santana, and I cashed
in my affirmative action
when he waited an extra
6 min for my baggage to
arrive.

La novia says
when I cut my hair to
a 0, I look 35% more
Chicano.
Adds an extra 10
if I put on a purple plaid
shirt.

What if you button the to—
Girl, don't even start.

Cont.

Ustedes

Tan learned. Tan
pinche learned.

(Apá, it's learn-ed.
¿No qué es lurn- duh?
Sí es, pero aquí,
you pronounce the
extra "ed." ¡Ay
puto inglés!)

In this context,
pinche
means "fucking."

Well not
"fuck" exactly, not
in the sexual sense.

Tiene más que ver
con exasperation.

Con estar desesperado
that you feel the need

to understand
everything

Cont.

Tú

Will spend three
quarters of the
time
commenting
on the use of
bilingualism.

Maybe this line's too
aggressive?

As if no other
aspect of craft
existed.

As if the poem is
too ethnic. You
know, like ethnic
ethnic.

Maybe you should
throw

some German,
quote Nietzsche,
or Husserl,
or Sartre,

or Lévi-Str—
Cont.

Saw 37 Latino
boys blend in Duke's
1,300+ Class of 2016,
and I thought
of the *Invisible Man* scene
at Liberty Paints Plant—

10 drops of black chemical
for "our white so white."

Papá asked if she needed
extra pillows for her back.

9 free hours now—

las llena con preguntas,
con,

"¿Qué quieres que te
prepare amor?"

She shuffles
tostada brands,
lava el apio twice, squeezes
la tortilladora,
the palm-pressed silver
kept from Cortés

and the boss
who just laid her off.

in this poem.
¡De Dolores,
cruzando la
frontera!

¡Tres días sin
comer, sin
agua, sin sins!

Su historia
is embalmed
in the
mahogany
varnish

of our 11 pm
dinner table.

And it will die

if I don't
write it.
And her back
hurts!

¡Hijos de la
chingada!

Is this poem
smarter now?

Can it be an
expat too? Can
it be abstract
too? Can
it *be* too?

Can *you* fix her
back?

¿Qué piensas?

¿Qué has
pensado? All
these centuries
. . .

(the tú is
informal).

"and the stars began to moan"

"A group of Dreamers . . . have been on a hunger strike since they were arrested Friday after a sit-in at the Capitol. The Dreamers are vowing to continue their hunger strike until Schumer and GOP Rep. Carlos Curbelo, R-Florida, win enough votes in the Senate and the House to delay a vote on the spending bill and force a vote on a clean DREAM Act."
—*CBS News*, December 18, 2017

Antonio López

AP US History

       Cuz our sky's full of ghosts,
dwarf madres que esperan eons
para sus papeles. Cruzaron

through the sunken night,
praying their moon
holds his sleep

under the Sonoran floodlight.

     ❡

       Porque las semillas del cielo
crecieron a ser ocho sentadores
who bursted on the pot

-bellied senadores of Capital
Hill. Who spore witness
to the perennial pendulum

of silk tiles, the cordless quiver
of budding interns—all the well
-fed stalks of careers rooted
in tilling a promise.

¶

Who morseled
on the cupped hands of mothers
that prayed under the shawls

of curtained homes. *Señor,*
cuide sus hijos que huelgan
en Wáchinton. Te lo ruego.

Her bearded sun rallies
an orbit of news cameras.
They zoom in on his head

-line, *They've taken so much*
from me. They've taken

my fear.

¶

After the vigil, I pour caldo
from la olla, its sides charred
from the restless chant

of flame. I kiss my hosts
as my parents once did theirs—
lift the crowned bowl

of thorny chayote, burnt papas,
yellowing limbs of leg
—their first American meal.

I salt the broth with my eyes,
taste the seasoned bones
I refuse to digest,

We could petition
and march until we wore
ourselves out, it would change
nobody's fate.

⸙

      Dear Jimmie,
watch as the seeds of Sonny
glow above their heads.

As you prophesized
in the last breath
of his blues,

the very cup of trembling.

Final: Magical Forrealism

V.
(35% of your worth)

Last section, pale strangers
fed you a language
of apostrophes—

a grammar of possession.
That is to say,
this book collapses

on one lesson:

to speak English
is to have an empire
flood your mouth.

Each word a scene
of subjection (Hartman 1997)
where men studded

your jaw, boasted to neighbors
its hollowed integrity—
how his history hung.

For this final project,
you will learn
to adapt: take
the mill that churned
your body. Swap it

for un molino—
the rusty corn-grinders
of Michoacán.

Stop renting this tongue,
and hotwire English itself,
the vehicle for mobility
that promised salvation.

Joyride their texts,
and redefine
the page's terms.

Magical Forrealism: To read of the ghosts
that haunted Macondo,
and see Moises' head
stapled to a telephone pole.
His moms in a white scarf
hands out flyers to the fat
paleteros stalked outside McNair.

Disculpe señor,
pero has visto—But he
just counts singles.
The boys whose hips
are already swollen
with dead presidents
and cold metal
the only children he sees.

Root: To take "Literature
of Latin America," and learn
you're Moises, still missing
from the syllabus. You ask
these white novelistas,
Where am I? No answer
but an essay where Octavio
calls you *a tangle of contradictions.*

First Known Use: 7th grade.
Ms. Nelson told the Mexican kids to stop speaking Spanish,
so I decided to live in the mouths of Devonte, Michael,
and the other black boys. Each a sanctuary city

to hide from detention. At recess, the blacktop
sweltered with ciphers. Lips like purple spigots leaked songs
from their Nokias. They beat their chests,

taut drums that must've nursed beats from the studio
apartments where knuckles met flesh.
When I recited their bars,

each word curved
as it left me—
like an exit wound.

from *Barrio Britannica*

God, Dios, Allah,

whatever tongue
speaks to you today,
see to it

que mi corazón sea un frasco,
overflowing with el agua
de los arroyos, the tears
de tu misericordia.

Convierte mi vientre
a un huehuetl, a drum,
to celebrate our union.
Melt this taut pottery
with Ibrahim's embers.

Coil my clay
so that I am ensnared
in your bosom.

Make my heart an oil stock
whose inner mesh clutches
onto the dregs of rosemary
inside the nave of Our Lady.

Where Mayan copal,
African frankincense,
Quetzal feathers, know
not why they can burn,

yet yearn to incinerate
themselves until the fragrance
reaches Your nose-mountains.

Rid me of Adán's obsession
to stake every plant and creature,
with Latin namesakes.

Que mi cuerpo sea un cirio
with an adobe shell that quietly
endures the heat of this dunya
enough to light this Basílica.

So God's children,
kings and beggars,
monjas y huríes
peasant and pope
can see each other's toes,

and keep the lines straight.

Tasbih, (I don't want this poem to be in English.)

I once called you rosario,
a crucifijo clenched
in the hand of Abuela

       whose lágrimas
       are a stuttering lluvia
       que cae al rancho. It cuts
       carretera stone, prays
       for the roadside skulls
       of drunken sons.

I want men to stop leaving her:
       for abuelo Güicho to rise
       from cerro-cemeterio. To lift
       his sombrero from the living
       room and wrap a handmade
       concha in his bandana—a token
       for the labores of Mictlán.

       To stop seeing grandchildren's English
       hit her face like the steam of store-bought Maizena.

       To take this poem
       and blanket her
       for winters in el norte.

I am afraid to join this male's betrayal, to open my palms and expose
       these polished orbs. Where I recite Allah's names:

Ar-Rahman, Ar-Rahim, Al-Malik. . . . I asked an imam,
　　What is the madhhab of Mexicans
　　who pray at the feet of a woman

whose hands jamás did not fold
　　for an absent man, and instead sunk
　　their nails in the corn's earth?
　　Who slabbed together tortillas
　　to feed her diez hijos, sang
　　to the mockingbirds perched
　　on thin chilitos?

The Gentle, before you call her too,

bless this tasbih that rattles
　　my neck.
Make me think of her every time
　　I hear its rain.

When Amá Asks Me, "¿Descríbeme Escuau?"
Community of Writers at Squaw Valley (July 28th, 2017)

¿Pus qué te diré?   Imagine
a giant raspado   atop the peaks.
Mango chunks of sunlight   glazing a granite cliff.

Montoya was right: God's an iceworker.
Grains of morena shaved off soggy styrofoam.
Aguas, he whispers, *se te entumirán las manos.*

Prueba su Tutti Frutti—you're tasting
an entire mountain.

Acá, if you sang in Squaw, no vecino
te reclamará. No, the night would take
off her starry earrings, desmaquillará
our city smog. Her naked breath
on your lips, *¿Dime hija, why so restless?*

Acá, the river's inquieta como tú.
Olas crash into one another
like two pairs of patas that scratch
each other in hangnail-fencing.

The epée mask sheets
of a living room mattress.
A match-cry, *¡Cochino,
córtate esas uñas!*

Acá, hay árboles for a million navidades.
Brushstrokes tan finas, parecen
the backdrop of a Sears album.

Acá, snow falls like queso cotija,
crumbles of México atop six-dollar china.

Acá, the cables of a ski lift bend
like homegirls' chicles. Mouths
stretch valles de plática. Tremors
of rubbery sap snap along jawline,

*"Ay Pati, deja contarte
de lo que él me dijo."*

They turn their necks sideways
like these A-frame edificios. Arches
second only to your strip mall cejas.

Mamá, if there was a telenovela here,
it'd be called *La Reina del Snow,*
name of the rickety iglesia
que paso on my way

to workshop, my greaser hands
stained by the anglo sludge
of anaphora y tercet,

y sé que you can't read the previous line.

Pero sepa: I'm always writing
to you.

Créemelo, I've waded through Squaw
long before mis tenis hit Reno,
this mile-high poesía where I inhale
an oxygen-thin industria.

Mamá, no quiero que te preocupes,
but this change in social elevation
me marea.

Mamá, can el frutero
teach me en-yamb-ment?

Mamá, can you proofread this grapevine chisme:
que daré a craft talk titled, "The Chicano Poet
Can't Spell Refrain without Efraín?"

Mamá, today a steel chafer handed
me his business card. Heated
my chest con promesas
de becas y residencias,
un libro with my last name.

But all I can see   is papá sirviéndome
across this table,   hands tightly folded
                           like restaurant napkins.

Mamá, here, I imagine your voice
beckons plumes de la galaxia.
God's milky ear trailing down
to the rhinestone-tacones

that stomp outside this deck.

El meadow tu micrófono.

As you teach me to sing
the nights without you.

First Time I Was Called a Spic

My mother pushes a stroller
above the freeway. Bar rayado
like the lottos that clog sewers.
Inside the port-a-cuna, un chango

munches on the last bits of a taco.
Corn flaps, dangling & sauced,
mock the pangs of hunger
in her stomach. The exhaust

of red taillights, white hoods, & blue
cielo will match the American flag
knitted on his sweatshirt.
The other Mexican boys drag

each other's mochilas, starched
shirts cologned by Papá's sweat.
Amá wipes chile from my cheek,
& kneels to me por la última vez.

My mother pushes a stroller
above the freeway. So I'd march
into Palo Alto, bearing our only oros
of a golden cross & golden arch.

Realtors on their second wind kept
the rest here, in houses we only enter
with hard hats. As Ms. G places
us in groups of four to five, I felt *her,*

the freckles on Ava's back. I pawed
its tawny pebbles, but my hands
slipped in the mud of her gleeful
burst, *I wish I had your tan.*

My mother pushes a stroller
above the freeway. So Mr. Matta
will slap me on the shoulder,
& shout in a Chilean mantra,

*Tony! I want you to go, because history
will speak of you.* Six of us fly
to the minority conference
in San Diego. & for the first time,

I feel beautiful by the sea of brown faces
that shores my grin. By the boardwalk,
I split a set of fries with the date
I met at the lunchtime talk.

We hide our skin in the border-
town's dusk, until she stops
& asks me to pick the palm
tree where she'll crop

her breath under my shirt.
The warm gusts coo my neck,
like a cobija freshly taken out
la secadora. With hands flecked,

I glide back to the hotel.
A man stands outside a bar.
Bubbles of Corona foam
from his mouth. He spars,

Got some Taco Bell huh? I volley
back, *Naw I think you buggin.*
It's Jack in the Box. With that
I've left the convent

of not talking back. He hisses
as I turn, *spic*. So the leash
against my neck can pull me
back to the curb, & teach

my children, & my children's
children, & my children's
children's children, to spend
their lives filling refreshments,

valeting his car at a finger's snap.
Mr. Matta charges for him, held back
by the other chaperones. The peach fuzz
boys & hair-straightened girls—name tags

still pinned—circle me & ask,
Hey Tony, are you ok? The tingling
comezón from swimming in mi ser
is drained. Siento encuerado, stinging

from the cudgels that chase me.
At that moment, I want to grab
my phone, & ask my mother,
How many times did you have

to cross that bridge?

Ya Es Hora (It's Nation Time Remix)
after Amiri Baraka

Ya es hora
de reunirnos. Put away
the saco and corbata politics.
Time to be one thick, picoso, mole.

Hora de levantar.
Ser.
Be
come. Ahora, para ser.

Que-

       Que-

              Que-

       Quetzalcoatl, descend
       to the underworld earth
       to retrieve from the bones
       of the Sonoran desert
       the fifth sun

of man who lies still grasping cuatrocientos ochenta y dos pesos
—it'd be five hundred but he spent eighteen munching
on stale papas fritas off a haggard street vendor—

¡Levántense! To be
the future of the world!
Brown folx is the future of the world!
Serás in 2050. Ciento seis. 106. Millones. Latinxs.
Be. Come.
Rise up. Wise up.

Son del brown feathered serpent
Son del viaje largo Ek Chuaj
Daughter of evil-warding machi
Daughter of Mama Killa's moon

     Move—
from mud brick back.
from Manco Cápac's golden staff
from ankle rattles and serpentine headdresses
from Fire Dance war drums and mortar aflame
       in the center.

     Hyea!!
Come out spics.
Drink your chicha, let the trance.

Trance.
     Trance.

Levántense levántense. Wake up earlier
than the fucking Mexicans
on Día de la Virgen.

Con tu burrito sabanero, sing
"Os pido posaadaaaa."
to the toppa tus lungs.

Your hijxs got the app for the I.C.E. checkpoints.
Time to "Pardon us. Pardon Us." Perdón que somos
once millones. De indocumentados. ¿Indocu-qué?

¿Cuántos? Spics in the back me oyen?! Once. Once.
Once you finish learning how to make the 't' sound,

*T*ell Goldman Sachs to pay
      los coyotes lo que nos falta.
*T*ell El Chapo we'll give 'em the money by Sunday.
      Citizen's arrest Mr. Pelos de Elote, pa' decirle que
      WE AIN'T GOIN NOWHERES, HOMES!
Go'head! Build that muro. Crown it with barbed wire.
      Give it a week & chu'll finna find
      belt buckles, tejanas, wedding dresses, soccer shoes, wallet photos
      wit a 13-digit phone number con the prefix 011 on the back,
      a clean pair of chones, pocket-sized patron saints,
      and a teenage girl with pelo lasio holding a sign that says,
      "Fuck weed.
      Legalize my mom!"

¡Sáltense! Xicanos. Boricuas. Peruanos. Guatamaltecos. Venezolanos
Afro/Chino/Árabe/Trans-
Chichen Itza-climbing, Orisha-chantin' paisanos.
No matter what you choose
to call yourselves, come out come out:
the half-white güero that checks Latino for a scholarship,
      but never shows up to a general body meeting;
the soul sister who can only speak
      Spanish from her hips;
the store clerk Margarita that speaks
      fluent broken English.

Come together un pueblo unido

Come out spics spics spics spics.
Come out come out.
It's nation time.
It's nation time.

Before the roaches finish
          the down payment for squatting
          in detention centers.
Before you need two proofs of residency
          to get a state ID.
Before they detain Wildin again.
Before they repeal DACA.
Before they quiet the queers' 1st Amendment rights.
Before a uterus is a threat to national security.
Before another "No Indictment."
Before Philando bleeds out
          on the shrugged shoulders of Facebook Live.
Before mi primo joins him.
Before stealing Swishers is justifiable homicide.
Before another Juan. Juantoomany. Juan should be
          enough for us to valer madre, no?!
Before they arrest the DREAMers.
Before Jaime loses his leg to diabetes.
Before picking up abuela Carmen from church.
Before the Qur'an is prison contraband.
Before, before, before.

Before the founding undocument,
recite the declaration:

We hold these truths to be self-evident,
that no human being is illegal.

When hermanos wanna stop asking
how to pronounce freedom,
come out spics spics.

Come out spics spics spics. Come out.
Help us stop the predator-in-chief.
Help us build a new world.

Spics come out, raza unida,
   as we link hands atop this Bestia.
   If we sleep, we slip to our deaths.

No se les olvide, as you approach
this prosperous country:
the tongues of your mothers
aren't on the currency exchange.

That we are the same, all shades of anger.
Come out spics come out.
Come out spics come out.

Oyes at this point idoncare just get up
and put on something!
'ámonos, we already mad late.

It's nation time eye ime.
   It's nation ti-eye ime.

It's nation time eye ime.
   It's nation ti-eye ime.
   Chant with the tamborazo
   It's nation time.

It's nation time, get up hermana!
   It's nation time. Build it.
   Get up Celia, pick up the Bata drums.
   Get up Selena, help her pick out a cute bra.
      "Que it's a bustieeeer!"
   Get up Norita, rifle the jungle's earth for the bones
   of our ballots.
   Get up Santo Romero, teach her how to shout her homilies.
   Get up C.L.R., tell her again that story about the island
   that shook the hemisphere.

C'mon!
Err'body's outside, esperándote.
Get up here, bow.
It's nation time.

Appendix

Antonio D. López
Parts of an Ese
Objective: American Letters
3 May, 2021

Admissions Statement

This ese resists/the urge to celebrate/for its own sake/subpoenas not archives or accolades/but the price paid.

When profiled/for a story, the ese ducks & flinches/partly outta instinct,/but mostly cuz I can't write/the word headshot/without it backfiring in my fingers.

What's the term/for a jammed metaphor,/for when err'y question inside the chamber/of a conference/feels loaded & heavy?

Here's a confession: I dream of an English/where I hear the word race/& see babies tumbling/down a meadow/their mothers downhill, arms shot up/from the earth/sleeves spilling with gaillardias.
This ese takes its inspiration from perennials,/tender saplings that die/& come back as if to teach us/how to press our ears to the earth/& hear the blossom./Oh I dream/of an English/where I hear race/& see not a field/day of trench coats/surround a mother, a shotgun/mic pressed to her face/black foam against a black cheek— the hour's softest thing.

I dream of a craft/where our backs aren't blurbed/for the parts that bleed/the richest.

The ese, unlike his uncles/doesn't lift lumber/or storage boxes/but hardbound backs inside the stacks of Stanford./The ese doesn't wait for a whistle/or a splintered phrase on the back/of a pickup/but a notification to ping my inbox./Mr. Lopez/Congratulations/*We are pleased to inform you that your manuscript/has been selected . . .* /We negotiate/my spine./I say 6 x 9/they reply all 6 x 7.

Here's the grand prize:/I am the first/of my bloodline to labor/ without lowering/my back.

The ese is partial heir/to the Library of Congress/y la Biblioteca Nacional/to those deathless words/poetry like bread./As in I'm tryna chase it/as in Neruda's dead/& I ain't tryna join him/for the state coroner to place/a white glove on my mom's shoulder/*it was cancer,* & she spends/the rest of her rest/in this life/to investigate how mines/ was ended, to exhume me/& lodged inside my ribcage she finds/an album titled *Los éxitos.*/& I am no longer son/but a soliloquy/of her singing/Rocío/in the garage/an endless loop/of *amor eterno.*

The ese is succession/to two generations:/one saw the poem/as a vehicle for revolution/the other's lived long enough/to teach it./ Together/they form a fence/that the ese's master/of hopping back & forth from./The ese's first master class he'll teach/is how I avoid the Spanish/word for success/cuz it reminds me/of exit: that leaving can also be/a kind of wounding./I've long abandoned/the wound-up notebooks/that we'd wait for Wal-Mart/to drop to 80 cents each/two full months/after back-to-school shopping.

I write on moleskins now/but every time I open them/I unearth bullet points.

I come from a country/which is this one/which spells success/for me differently./As how often I wear a suit/outside a court date/or how I wait for my sentence/not forced to stand.//I am captive/only to my imagination.//The ese was raised/by a school of thought/where boys bruised each other/into softness./Where tender/meant a beating/or a bill tucked/inside a concealed thigh.

The ese's origin story is as follows:/once upon a time, a Mexican boy/ got tired of seeing magazines/kill his friends/so one day, he picked up a BiC & held his own locked-up/imagination at ballpoint.

He said, *write.*/Said, *right.*/Said, *rite.*/& slowly, the cold steel/became light/in his fingers/& the 2.6 lbs/that slayed scores of saints/was pawn-swapped for a mag/weighing oz's, bought back/not from the PD/but *Poets & Writers.*//The catch was I still had/to feed the beast lead/dub it No. 2/for the sake of memory/which is a poetic way/of saying what you ain't/been able to forget.//The deal didn't bring 'em back/but at least now my boys bleed/in the whitest gloss.

This ese dreams to be judged/by a jury of its peers/so it sneaks them under/a thin blanket of wordplay. The ese makes limón ada/outta lemonade, shops/at Ross—gay/is what Marcel/& the rest of my classmates scoffed/whenever one of us/called a girl cute/not fine/—or Marshalls, Nate/Dogg blasts in his trunk/his Cutlass cruising/down the cul de sac.//As final image, the ese corrals/the neighbors who eddy/round the whip/& straight out the dome/he remixes *Guillotine*/ to feature Gucci Mane/*his beard an avalanche*/*of [money]*/*BRR!!!!*

Behind the black bars/of my/poems Polys break the line/of scrimmage, finishing/their last Rugby play./Shout out to all my Razorbacks/who after the game/ordered 40 McChickens/y la cajera 'hind the counter/pobrecita, her uñas/tapping in iambic./After all, to survive/is a kind of rhyming./She's tryna to keep up/with the player's mouth./& seeing mines drop the floor,/he cheesed *Oh, dis for the team,*/& suddenly I 'membered/the koan of classmates://are Samoans & Tongans/jus supersized Mexicans,/or are we/jus a value-version/of them?

& bromas aside/y'all ever seen a haka/in the middle of a sideshow?/
Or a #JusticeForBreonnaTaylor march/stop incoming traffic/on the
corner of Garden & Clarke/dancing to the live banda/that brasses
in somejuan's one story?/& behind the picket fence/paisas salute the
picket signs/no longer resigned/or reclined/on plastic chairs,/but
standing—lil' wobbly I'll admit/but that's more from the palomas/
than political stance./Puedes ver/the sun bleeding/through the holes
of sombreros?/Can you hear/as they cheer on/the feet que zapatean/
the asphalt/a flurry of Air Forces/& huaraches?&/Do you spot the
homie/in a wheelchair/doin donuts/with his free hand/the other
holding a blunt?/See the officers/stand down, monitoring/the march's
front flank? Hear the megaphone/resume a song/that's been sampled/
since 1619.//& somewhere in this street/a newborn & a grown
man/both newly arrived to this land/learn their first words/in this
language/*No Justice, No Peace.*

& behold, my beautiful fucking city/how for decades, the only health
care we had/was each other. Till Zuckerberg/gained face, booked out
the rest/of his Fri appts/to ribbon cut/a couple millies/& the other
businessmen/followed suit, so strokes/of pen later, mothers stopped
getting check-ups/in beige portables, & I can still feel/my Skechers
light up the wheelchair ramp/of the WIC office./I still hear/its hollow
ring/as my mother asks the nutrition assistant/which brands of milk
we can buy/& all it costs, she said, is a long line/at Safeway, for
the lady behind us/to kiss her pearly whites & move/to the express
checkout./But we are too busy to realize/we're stereotypes/as we watch
the conveyer belt out/our bounty: a block of cheese/frozen cans of
orange juice/the food-wrapped voice/of Amá/still packed inside.

For further explanation/of this metaphor, see Baldwin/who is pacing
across the raised platform/of this ese, his right hand's/inside his dress
pants, not quite/in a fist, but cocked./Inside Cambridge Union/he's

delivering the final blow/to a civilization/its professed innocence/*I am not a ward of America,/I am not an object of missionary charity.*/The debate in question/is if this nation,/its myth & might,/is all at the expense/of a single tithe/& perhaps this/is what *Gentefication*/sought to do:/to write back/to the struggle/that made mines possible.

My ex-peers/who while I honed sentences/in Jersey, started a lifelong one./Mi abuela/who couldn't afford/la prepa her hija wanted/so err'y time Mom peered/into my room/she'd simply close the door/whenever the noise in the house/would bother me/but not before scanning/my desk, an IKEA hand-me-brown/& the big BIOLOGY textbook/the leopard on its cover/lazily gazing skyward.

This ese stands from his chair & opens the door/his father peers/from beneath the blanket/before stepping out the pick up/that carried him/& his brothers/across./How hours later/he saw it/the safehouse/the bucket of KFC, where pieces/of men gather, fried/from a week's worth of sunlight/& with shaking hands/I imagine them/tearing up/las tortillas/that like them, sweat/from hiding beneath cloth.

I imagine them/bowed in silence/just as their wives/& mothers were/inside the village church./My grandmother hobbles/up the hill to relay the message/¡he called, he called!/The call will be brief/*I was on a train, I love you too/the coyote almost left us/how is my mother/yes we just ate,/by the second train, the women broke down/the priest in Hermosillo blessed us/on the bus/warned us not to cross, said* don't, please don't. *Pickup truck/blanket was so itchy/and heavy/I held/my breath/Meño got nervous./Remember when we were kids, Hermanito/just like that/you're doing great/radio static, desert/the sound of tires/crushing bone/desert, heat, here/what even is here/I don't know/yet/I'll write soon/God first.*

& on the seventh day/he reaches a city/of angels. Today/is the 4th of July/1982, a new day/of independence. Today/is the 15th of September, 2021/day of my book launch/start of a heritage month/now called Latino/or Latinx/or prolly something else/in five years./Day of fireworks/of wrinkled flags/of flyers & bright-light marquees./Of leaving México/lindo y lejano/of me/flying into Manhattan/to read these poems/like a G/on economy plus.

This ese looks out the window/thinking of all it took/to get him here.

Notes

"Course Description"—The image in this poem was originally drawn up by radical cartographer William Rankin, an academic based at Yale University who maps everything from subways to whole cities. The map of East Palo Alto was found on arcgis.com.

"sideshow" is a mash-up of Danez Smith's "genesissy" with E-40's Bay Area classic "Tell Me When to Go."

"Letter to the Editor" cites an actual 2015 article by Dara Kerr titled, "East Palo Alto: Life on the Other Side of Silicon Valley's Tracks" published by C|Net.

"The Hadith of Gabriel" references a famous hadith (narration) of Gabriel to the Prophet Muhammad (PBUH), where the archangel asks him four questions to test his knowledge about Islam.

"Convert Glossary" is inspired by *Fortress of the Muslim,* a pocket-sized book of invocations commonly given to new members of the faith.

The section "Document-Based Questions" references the national AP US History exam conducted by the College Board. Its structure consists of a series of primary sources, usually concerning a particular time period, followed by an essay question that the student must answer in an allotted time.

"Magical Forrealism"—The poem's quoted phrase, "tangle of contradictions," is in reference to an essay in Octavio Paz's *Labyrinth of Solitude*, "The Pachuco and Other Extremes" (1953).

Shout-outs

Hay tanta gente que tengo que agradecer. The village can't fit in this white space I inherited as an Amerikan writer. But let me take a lesson from the smuggler lurking border towns and pack my people across the barbed margins of the written page.

For this, I must first thank my older sister Lupita, the Holmes to my Hamish Watson, the homegirl who can recite more lines than Homer. In my daydreams at Oxford, I run through aisles of joy with you, those of our late-night runs to Safeway hungry to fill our bellies with 2-for-$4.99 Cheetos.

Before I ever felt seen on the page, I felt seen with you.

To Angela and Aaron, mis hermanitos—I'm sorry that I've been away. The tuition for my eight years of higher ed wasn't in dollars, but in days of absence. I am sorry for missing so many memories: elementary school recitals, losing baby teeth, driving practice. I take solace in the fact that on holiday breaks, when you see me gerrymander the kitchen room table with stacks of books, seeing my unabashed nerdiness makes your aspirations just a bit realer. Recuerden este idioma que nuestros padres pasaron a nosotros.

Para mis papás, Antonio López & Luisa Méndez,
que jamás soñaron que iban a recoger un poemario
escrito por uno de sus hijos.

And that I always write to and for you.

To María Mendez, mi prima-hermana—thank you for coming back to our lives. Your laughter in the living room as you and the girls gossip is my favorite background music.

Te llevo dentro mi corazón.

I am grateful for my English teachers: Darice Elmore who handled 32 Brown and Black 8th graders in that packed classroom in East Palo Alto, who taught us the appositive with an overhead projector whose chinked glass ran a long gash on the wall.

Who in words, never let me feel poor.
Whose lesson plans under her desk's piles of manila could have very well been titled, "How to Make Them Feel this Language is Theirs."

To Rebecca Gertmenian who first read my essays about leaving a Title I school to attend a leading college prep in the Bay Area, who said, "Tony, this is beautiful," who made me feel beautiful in words, who inspired me to send this assignment for AP American Lit to *TeenInk,* the nation's leading magazine for adolescents and my first publication, who gave me a dog-eared copy of *Hunger of Memory,* thank you. I awed over reading an author with a last name that rhymed with mine, whose bio read like a prophecy, "He begins his schooling in Sacramento, California, knowing just 50 words of English, and concludes his university studies in the stately quiet of the reading room of the British Museum."

Ms. Gertmenian, I am writing these words in a painting room at Oxford.

To Mark Clevenger, my college counselor and creative writing teacher in 12th grade, who put down my personal statements and said, "You have a bright future ahead of you," who personally picked out Julia Alvarez's *A Wedding in Haiti* when I won the school's Muse Award which dubbed me, "The Essayist," who paid for my SAT and college application fees, who used his Delta miles to fly me to Duke's orientation week.

To the White people who were allies in the process of me seeing my own humanity.

Thank you Peter Moore, whose "Introduction to Poetry" my sophomore year at Duke gave me my first dips into this craft. I have to doubly thank him for pulling me aside from the weight room, and saying, "Look man I'm telling you. Take Nate's class." And months later, I met Nathaniel Mackey. His "Advanced Poetry" course was my first experience into a workshop setting. He sat me down one day after class, held my poems in the air, and asked, "Do you know the work of Juan Felipe Herrera? No? How about

Lorna Dee Cervantes? Oh come on man, these are your people!"

And after reading *Emplumada* and *Border-Crosser with a Lamborghini Dream,* I knew my life would be in letters.
And speaking of letters, I am grateful for three of them Rutgers-Newark gave me: MFA. From Melissa Hartman helping us sort our lives, to the world-class faculty that taught me in and out the classroom, 43 Bleeker was a wonderful place. To Alice Dark, Brenda Shaughnessy, John Keene, Tayari Jones, A. Van Jordan, Akhil Sharma, James Goodman, and Jayne Anne Phillips, thank you.

And of course, my cohort, the dopest poets on the planet. Shout out to Cheswayo Mphanza and Dimitri Reyes, my two near and dear brothers in poetry. What a gift it was to have you both for those two years. In all our hangouts, we sought to teach each other what it means to be men of color in this space.

I look forward to posing on all the red carpets.

You made workshop feel like home.

Salute to the rest of the MFA family during my time there (in no particular order): Musa Syeed, Shara Davis, Tracy Fuad, Simeon Marsalis, Ariel Yelen, Sam Hutchings, Nadia Choudhry, Amy Dougher, Alegra Padron, Emily Luan, An Li, Susanna Covarrubias, Grey Vild, Andy Gallagher, and Bronwyn Douman who said to me after my KGB reading, "Every time I hear your poetry, I want to fight." Another round of thanks to Emily Caris, Jodi Manjourides, Joshua Irwin, Karen May, Lauren Parrot, Madini Sheikh, Maia Morgan, Martina Fouquet, Mary Kouth, Nhu Xuân Nguyễn, Ricardo Hernandez, and Thierry Kehou.

I'll always cherish the conversations I had with these writers, whether they took place at the ritzy jazz-lounge of Clement's Place at 15 Washington St, or over a few pints at McGovern's.

Muchísimas gracias to the faculty and staff at the Community of Writers at Squaw Valley. To Brett Hall Jones, Laura Howard, Eva Melas,

Kaitlin Klaussen, thank you. Your Lucille Clifton Memorial Scholarship in summer of 2017 gave me the financial means to cultivate and share my work in my first professional workshop. It was the confidence I needed a year into my MFA.

To Tin House, whose scholarship the subsequent year made possible my attendance for a workshop with Danez Smith. To Danez Smith!

Danez Smith, who when I announced on social media that I'd won the prize that made this book possible, tweeted,

> This poet? One of my favorite poets I've had the pleasure of having in workshop. Can't wait for the world to be blessed by this joint. It's [fire emoji] [sparkle] [bugged out face] [golden heart] [crying] [heart-eyed] [eyes peepin] [black power fist] [head exploding].

Danez, your books are bibles for me. I am always writing alongside you. Danez, PS: there are two things in this world that make me cry the most: you rereading "Somewhere, Summer" in American wilderness of Portland, and listening to Rocío Dúrcal's "Amor eterno."

To my fellow 2018 Summer Workshop Scholars who I met and loved along the way: first to Jesús Valles, your book is next mi chula; Threa Almontaser, you and DMX are my favorite poets from Yonkers; Destiny Birdsong, Tin House is so blessed to house your debut; Allison Albino, the sweetest and most loving soul I've met. Your long form on the page is a feast I never want to put down; Dantiel Moniz; Nathan Go; Sacha Idell; Cassandra Lopez, that poem of the police raid eating soup at a Mexican home still haunts me; Monterica Sade Neil, a whole-ass prodigy of the memoir, our generation's Kiese Laymon; Manuel Martinez; Margaret Meehan; Luke Muyskens; David Sanchez, Eva Speer; Keith S. Wilson, as badass as you are, I still remember you as my hallmate who rocked the Starcraft t-shirt; Jenna Wortham; Joaquin Zihuatanejo, the world slam champ who gave me a ride to the Portland Safeway to get shampoo.

A thanks también to the Tin House staff whose scholarship allowed me to attend the Portland conference in the first place. It was an honor to be share community at the Sequoia House with some of the most brilliant writers of my generation.

To Lance Cleland, for shepherding one of the most progressive writing workshops in the country. As the saying goes, y'all know what's up. To Camille Dungy, who advocated for my poetry to be in *Tin House Magazine*'s last issue, who said on the car ride back to our rooms, "Why not a PhD at Stanford?"

Camille, by the time these words are in print, I will be in my second year at Stanford's Modern Thought and Literature program. Thank you.

To the folks at the 2017 Santa Barbara Writers' Conference, to Perie Longo and especially Laure-Anne Bosselaar, my adopted White abuela. What a gift to have been your student, to have had your constant words of affirmation, "Pease please keep writing Antonio." Two years and an award-winning book later, here we are. I love you so much Laure-Anne!

To the Macondo Writers Workshop, who reminded me that it is not simply enough to write, but do right, as in derecho, who reminded me of the rich Latinx literary community I hail from. To Sandra Cisneros, its founder. To the Macondistas I met there, but especially Jesus Mena, a man whose activism in the 60s inspires me to work in this beautiful but fraught tradition of Chicanidad. To Allison Hedge Cooke, and my fellow workshop participants: Natalia Treviño, Angela Peñaredondo, Melissa Bennett, Xochitl-Julisa Bermejo, Cecilia Macias-McCardle, Juan J. Morales, Sabrina San Miguel, Karla Cordero, Gerardo Pachecho, and Willy Palomo. Mil gracias.

A special thanks to Laura Villareal, a fellow Rutgers MFA'er from '17, who on the eve of our open mic night at San Antonio, told me, "You're ready for a book." For nicknaming me "Tío" for all my avuncular mannerisms, I say gracias.

And a special thank you to Willy Palomo for taking the time to review this manuscript when it was inching towards completion. You were its perfect reader. Thank for agüantando so many back-and-forth emails, for giving me the critical feedback I needed to get before sending this book out to the world. I knew we'd be kindred spirits ever since we broke tortillas at that restaurant in San Antonio.

Pase lo que pase, I got mad love for you.

And speaking of love, thank you to Janel Pineda—for yours, for your patience and care in reviewing parts of these poems, for your countless affirmations to prioritize my work even when I don't. And most of all, for sharing your light and life with me.

To Rigoberto González, gracias profe, for writing all those letters of rec, for being honest about my work when I needed to hear it, for fighting for me when I didn't know how to fight for myself. For telling me, "You really are the son of Juan Felipe Herrera."

Rigo, you are our greatest champion in Chicanx letters. Sabes, you are a proverbial godfather, dunking so many of our heads inside fonts of the canon. So many communities are indebted to you.

And to my thesis adviser, Cathy Park Hong, who reminded me that telling our stories as people of color isn't enough. Who wants a revolution like me, who says we need to push this form for the sake of our radical imaginations, who is ready to throw intellectual hands at folks who refuse to see how we're changing the game. Cathy, it was the honor of a lifetime to have you read the earliest (and most humbling) parts of this draft. It's a blessing to have so many people tell me, "You do that thing she does in *Dance Dance Revolution.*"

What a gift it is to talk across diasporas with you.

To Greg Pardlo, for tolerating this dense-ass manuscript, for replying to my longwinded thanks over email, "It's a good book homie." To Martha Rhodes, for entertaining my excitement over phone calls. To Ryan Murphy, Clarissa Long, and all the good folks at Four Way Books for giving my first book a home.

For letting me call Rigo and Laure-Anne my pressmates. Qué bendición, la neta.

Reader, indulge me una última vez, and let me lay out for you the day I heard I won the Larry Levis Prize. (I do so because I want to demystify my trajectory, to tell you, más bien tell myself, that all of this is possible.)

It was August 20, 2019, and day 6 of the Bread Loaf Conference, where I was the recipient of the Katherine Bakeless Prize. I just finished reading "Conjugations of My Tía's Back" to a packed audience at the Little Theater. And man, people roared and cheered so loudly, I thought the lights above me would shatter. A file of folks came to embrace me— workshop participants, literary agents, Kevin Young, to whom I said in rare braggadocio, "Expect a poem of mine to *the New Yorker* soon."

Then, a hand grabs my shoulder. It's Alexander Chee, who in his sweet tenor said, "We have to celebrate. Let me pour you a drink back at the writers' house."

Twenty minutes later, as Alexander shovels ice into a Dixie cup, I watch Jericho Brown and Kevin playing cards on the table. I have to pinch myself in knowing that tomorrow, and the next day, and the next day, and the day after that, I will sit next to Jericho at workshop. I break focus, and see Jenny Xu, the associate from Houghton Mifflin Harcourt, holding a cup of her own.

And at that moment, I replayed how earlier that day, at our 1:00 agent meeting, I had given Jenny a printed version of my manuscript, which was available for about 54 minutes, because at 1:54 PM, while sitting at a craft class on writing about neighborhoods, I checked my phone (big mistake) and saw an email with the subject headline, "Antonio, Great News." It was Martha writing that I had won the prize, the first paragraph ending with "If you were elated at the news of being a finalist, you will be off the charts... Gregory Pardlo has selected . . Gentefication . . . winner of the 2019 . . . Prize in Poetry. Sit down. Take a breath."

Flashbacked to this writers' house, I excuse myself from Jenny and do just that. I sit down on the room's couch, but next to me is Vievee Francis! Vievee! My heart is zapateando at this point, but I do my very mortal best to muster up a casual conversation. But all that flows from my mouth is how much I loved her reading, her odes to the four Black girls inside that

Birmingham church. She smiled, flattered. I don't remember much of the conversation, but I do recall her looking at me and saying, "I'm glad this place is making some good changes 'round here."

I nod, liquor-headed. I lift the Dixie and make a solo toast to Jennifer Grotz.

I leave Vievee too, then walk up to the corner where the card game unfolds. I sit on the windowsill and watch the spades and clubs being slammed.

Paul Tran is next to me, with their characteristic smirk. It is a welcome without the words. And with the brown in my eyes, I thank them for being here. I stare through the window that now grazes my shoulder, look out into the sprawling hills of Vermont darkened by night, the meadows I ran that afternoon with joy at that day's news, and think to myself,

"This life, this life is truly mine."

And so, a final thank you to all my Chicanxs, South Central Americans, Latinxs of all shades; to all my Black Americans, American Africans, all hopscotchers of the hyphen; to all my queer and trans and displaced migrants; to the womxn who raised me, and who still teach me; to the men of color present in our lives: this book is for you.

May you go out and write yours,

Antonio D. López
Oxfordshire, England
January 2020

P.S. To all the presses, publications & blogas that took a shot at my shit from day one, good looking.

Poetry Northwest, Track//Four: Sinking City Lit Mag:
Puerto del Sol, BOAAT Press: Entropy, Red Wheelbarrow Press,
Lunch Ticket, Reconstructed Magazine, Dryland,
The ISIS Magazine, Gramma Press: Cosmonauts Avenue:
The New Republic, La Bloga, Free State Review,

After Happy Hour Review, Arcturus Review, Grist Journal, and *Huizache.*

Born and raised in East Palo Alto, CA, Antonio López has received scholarships to attend the Community of Writers at Squaw Valley, Tin House, the Vermont Studio Center, and Bread Loaf. He is a proud member of the Macondo Writers Workshop and a CantoMundo Fellow. He holds degrees from Duke University, Rutgers-Newark, and the University of Oxford. He is pursuing a PhD in Modern Thought and Literature at Stanford University. His debut poetry collection, *Gentefication,* was selected by Gregory Pardlo as the winner of the 2019 Levis Prize in Poetry. Antonio is currently fighting gentrification in his hometown as the newest and youngest councilmember for the City of East Palo Alto.

Publication of this book was made possible by grants and donations. We are also grateful to those individuals who participated in our 2020 Build a Book Program. They are:

Anonymous (14), Robert Abrams, Nancy Allen, Maggie Anderson, Sally Ball, Matt Bell, Laurel Blossom, Adam Bohannon, Lee Briccetti, Therese Broderick, Jane Martha Brox, Christopher Bursk, Liam Callanan, Anthony Cappo, Carla & Steven Carlson, Paul & Brandy Carlson, Renee Carlson, Cyrus Cassells, Robin Rosen Chang, Jaye Chen, Edward W. Clark, Andrea Cohen, Ellen Cosgrove, Peter Coyote, Janet S. Crossen, Kim & David Daniels, Brian Komei Dempster, Matthew DeNichilo, Carl Dennis, Patrick Donnelly, Charles Douthat, Morgan Driscoll, Lynn Emanuel, Monica Ferrell, Elliot Figman, Laura Fjeld, Michael Foran, Jennifer Franklin, Sarah Freligh, Helen Fremont & Donna Thagard, Reginald Gibbons, Jean & Jay Glassman, Ginny Gordon, Lauri Grossman, Naomi Guttman & Jonathan Mead, Mark Halliday, Beth Harrison, Jeffrey Harrison, Page Hill Starzinger, Deming Holleran, Joan Houlihan, Thomas & Autumn Howard, Elizabeth Jackson, Christopher Johanson, Voki Kalfayan, Maeve Kinkead, David Lee, Jen Levitt, Howard Levy, Owen Lewis, Jennifer Litt, Sara London & Dean Albarelli, David Long, James Longenbach, Excelsior Love, Ralph & Mary Ann Lowen, Jacquelyn Malone, Donna Masini, Catherine McArthur, Nathan McClain, Richard McCormick, Victoria McCoy, Ellen McCulloch-Lovell, Judith McGrath, Debbie & Steve Modzelewski, Rajiv Mohabir, James T. F. Moore, Beth Morris, John Murillo & Nicole Sealey, Michael & Nancy Murphy, Maria Nazos, Kimberly Nunes, Bill O'Brien, Susan Okie & Walter Weiss, Rebecca Okrent, Sam Perkins, Megan Pinto, Kyle Potvin, Glen Pourciau, Kevin Prufer, Barbara Ras, Victoria Redel, Martha Rhodes, Paula Rhodes, Paula Ristuccia, George & Nancy Rosenfeld, M. L. Samios, Peter & Jill Schireson, Rob Schlegel, Roni & Richard Schotter, Jane Scovell, Andrew Seligsohn & Martina Anderson, James & Nancy Shalek, Soraya Shalforoosh, Peggy Shinner, Dara-Lyn Shrager, Joan Silber, Emily Sinclair, James Snyder & Krista Fragos, Alice St. Claire-Long, Megan Staffel, Bonnie Stetson, Yerra Sugarman, Dorothy Tapper Goldman, Marjorie & Lew Tesser, Earl Teteak, Parker & Phyllis Towle, Pauline Uchmanowicz, Rosalynde Vas Dias, Connie Voisine, Valerie Wallace, Doris Warriner, Ellen Doré Watson, Martha Webster & Robert Fuentes, Calvin Wei, Bill Wenthe, Allison Benis White, Michelle Whittaker, and Ira Zapin.